Christmas Eve

The Nativity Story
in Engravings, Verse, and Song

Gibbs Smith, Publisher
Salt Lake City

First Edition
09 08 07 06 05   5 4 3 2 1

Inspired by a handmade book by Carole Taylor
Text from the King James Version of the Bible

Original engravings © 2005 Lezle Williams
Music arrangements © 2005 Robert J. Holub

Original signed engravings from this book and other art available at
www.laughingcrowstudio.com

Published by
Gibbs Smith, Publisher
P.O. Box 667
Layton, Utah 84041

Orders: 1.800.748.5439
www.gibbs-smith.com

Designed by Kurt Wahlner and Sheryl Dickert Smith
Printed and bound in the United States of America

ISBN 1-58685-830-0

O, Come All Ye Faithful

THE VIRGIN MARY

Leslie Williams

And in the sixth month the angel
Gabriel was sent from God unto a city of
Galilee, named Nazareth,

To a virgin espoused to a man whose name was
Joseph, of the house of David; and the virgin's
name was Mary.

And the angel said unto her, Fear not, Mary:
for thou hast found favour with God.

And, behold, thou shalt conceive in thy womb,
and bring forth a son, and shalt call his name
JESUS.

He shall be great, and shall be called the Son of
the Highest.

Luke 1:26–27, 30–32

And it came to pass in those days, that there went out a decree from Caesar Augustus, that all the world should be taxed.

And all went to be taxed, every one into his own city.

And Joseph also went up from Galilee, out of the city of Nazareth, into Judaea, unto the city of David, which is called Bethlehem;

To be taxed with Mary his espoused wife, being great with child.

LUKE 2:1, 3-5

ENTERING BETHLEHEM

Leslie Williams

O Little Town of Bethlehem

And so it was, that, while they were there, the days were accomplished that she should be delivered.

And she brought forth her firstborn son, and wrapped him swaddling clothes, and laid him in a manger; because there was no room for them in the inn.

LUKE 2:6-7

AWAY IN THE MANGER

Leslie Williams

Away in a Manger

And there were in the same country shepherds abiding in the field, keeping watch over their flock by night.

And, lo, the angel of the Lord came upon them, and the glory of the Lord shone round about them: and they were sore afraid.

LUKE 2:8–9

SHEPHERDS IN THE FIELD   Leslie Williams

And the angel said unto them, Fear not: for, behold, I bring you good tidings of great joy, which shall be to all people.

For unto you is born this day in the city of David a Saviour, which is Christ the Lord.

And this shall be a sign unto you; Ye shall find the babe wrapped in swaddling clothes, lying in a manger.

And suddenly there was with the angel a multitude of the heavenly host praising God, and saying,

Glory to God in the highest, and on earth peace, good will toward men.

LUKE 2:10–14

It Came Upon a Midnight Clear

HARK! THE HERALD ANGELS SING

And it came to pass, as the angels were gone away from them into heaven, the shepherds said one to another, Let us now go even unto Bethlehem, and see this thing which is come to pass, which the Lord hath made known unto us.

And they came with haste, and found Mary, and Joseph, and the babe lying in a manger.

LUKE 2:15–16

Silent Night

THE SHEPHERDS' VISIT

And when they had seen it, they made known abroad the saying which was told them concerning this child.

And all they that heard it wondered at those things which were told them by the shepherds.

But Mary kept all these things, and pondered them in her heart.

And the shepherds returned, glorifying and praising God for all the things that they had heard and seen, as it was told unto them.

Luke 2:17-20

The First Noel

Now when Jesus was born in Bethlehem of Judaea in the days of Herod the king, behold, there came wise men from the east to Jerusalem,

Saying, Where is he that is born King of the Jews? for we have seen his star in the east, and are come to worship him.

When Herod the king had heard these things, he was troubled, and all Jerusalem with him.

Then Herod, when he had privily called the wise men, enquired of them diligently what time the star appeared.

And he sent them to Bethlehem, and said, Go and search diligently for the young child; and when ye have found him, bring me word again, that I may come and worship him also.

MATTHEW 2:1–3, 7–8

HEROD'S PALACE

Leslie Williams

When they had heard the king, they departed; and, lo, the star, which they saw in the east, went before them, till it came and stood over where the young child was.

When they saw the star, they rejoiced with exceeding great joy.

And when they were come into the house, they saw the young child with Mary his mother, and fell down, and worshipped him: and when they had opened their treasures, they presented unto him gifts; gold, and frankincense, and myrrh.

And being warned of God in a dream that they should not return to Herod, they departed into their own country another way.

MATTHEW 2:9–12

FOLLOWING THE STAR

Lisle Williams

We Three Kings

And when they were departed, behold, the angel of the Lord appeareth to Joseph in a dream, saying, Arise, and take the young child and his mother, and flee into Egypt, and be thou there until I bring thee word: for Herod will seek the young child to destroy him.

When he arose, he took the young child and his mother by night, and departed into Egypt:

And was there until the death of Herod: that it might be fulfilled which was spoken of the Lord by the prophet, saying, Out of Egypt have I called my son.

MATTHEW 2:13–15

ESCAPE TO NAZARETH

Leslie Williams

But when Herod was dead, behold, an angel of the Lord appeareth in a dream to Joseph in Egypt,

Saying, Arise, and take the young child and his mother, and go into the land of Israel: for they are dead which sought the young child's life.

And he arose . . . and he came and dwelt in a city called Nazareth.

MATTHEW 2:19–20, 21, 23

CITY OF NAZARETH

Leslie Williams

And the child grew, and waxed strong in spirit, filled with wisdom: and the grace of God was upon him.

LUKE 2:40

JOY TO THE WORLD